Gospels From the Lower Shelf

poems by

Thomas Dukes

Finishing Line Press
Georgetown, Kentucky

Gospels From the Lower Shelf

Copyright © 2024 by Thomas Dukes
ISBN 979-8-88838-705-4 First Edition
All rights reserved under International and Pan-American Copyright Conventions. No part of this book may be reproduced in any manner whatsoever without written permission from the publisher, except in the case of brief quotations embodied in critical articles and reviews.

ACKNOWLEDGMENTS

I thank Elton Glaser and Lynn Powell for their help in my writing this book. I also owe much to Diana Reep, Mary Biddinger, Jana Russ, and Janet Marting for their tireless encouragement and suggestions. I am grateful to the Poets and Writers' League of Greater Cleveland/The Lit, the Sandhills' Writers Conference, and the Wayne College Regional Writing Awards for their support.

Publisher: Leah Huete de Maines
Editor: Christen Kincaid
Cover Art: Andrew Le
Author Photo: Andrew Le
Cover Design: Elizabeth Maines McCleavy

Order online: www.finishinglinepress.com
also available on amazon.com

Author inquiries and mail orders:
Finishing Line Press
PO Box 1626
Georgetown, Kentucky 40324
USA

Contents

One

A Horticulturalist's Guide to Marriage in Ohio 1
Lambing 2
Etudes for El Paso and Spanish Guitar 3
Personal Testimony 7
Letters from the Gay Menopause House of Detention
    and Eternal Prayer 9
Lost in the Art of Mary Cassett 11
For the Queens Who Dragged Marlene's Furs Across my Life 13
October in Richfield, Ohio 14
Ohio is Where I Hang 15
Gentlemen of a Certain Age Perform Your Broadway Favorites 16
Poem for my Nightstand 18
Queer Body 19
Coyotes Walk Up Oakdale Street on Christmas Eve 20
Daddy Fishing at Whittle's Pond 22

Two

Camp Meeting 25
Hawk in December 27
Gospels from the Lower Shelf 28
Idol Worship 31
Abiding Light 32
Mrs. Bendremer 33
Odella, At Eighty 34
Son, Watermelon Should Be Blood Red 35
Education 36
Stealing Lumber on a Sunday Afternoon 37
Barrier Island Lullaby for 3 a.m. 38
Try Me 39
My Buddy 40
Walking the Moon at 3 a.m. 42

Three

Genuine Antics for Sale 45

Guys with Their Hands in Their Pockets 47
A Woman Bathes in the Ohio River on Sunday Afternoon 48
Red Onions 50
Ohio Farm Boy 51
Ruth Speaks at the Buckeye Jewish Center Adult Tap Class 52
Baptists in Oberlin 53
Miss Cleveland Drag 1979 Packs Away Liza Forever 54
I Need from You an Advisement 55
January in the Ohio River Valley 57
Many Bright Mansions Above 58

Four

Goose Up a Tree at Beaver Marsh 61
Knives 62
A Mary Cassatt Suite 63
Beagle 66
The Only Time I Wished I Were Straight 67
Marriage Blanc 69
New Thinking on How to Protect the Heart 70
The Sewing Circle and Altar Guild of St. Michael's
   Episcopal Church 71
Before the Rapture Comes 72
Brandywine Falls in June 73
Blackberry Summer 74
Bowls 75
Akron Rain in Late Middle Age 76
Tibetan Prayer Flags in Holmes County, Ohio 78

Notes 79

for Diana, Peggy, and Rich

One

I turn my face away from
Anything that might display
The broken lover or dilapidated boy,

How can I like what looks back at me,
The eccentric replicas,
Vanity reversed across the glass,

—Elton Glaser, "Pixelated"

A Horticulturalist's Guide to Marriage Equality in Ohio

> *My beloved has gone down to his garden, to the bed of spices*
> Song of Solomon 6:2

In the everyday soil of my complaints,
    Rich set three Carolina hydrangeas because
Mama grew them with heads big as planets:
    the people who bought her house
chopped up Eden before the bank foreclosed,
    and I lost Mama a second time.

Each summer Rich drops zinnias in lavender rows
    of twenty-one, plus a few colorblind patches,
gambling that their bowed heads can survive
    Ohio's roulette of moles, groundhogs,
and other arguments with the stormy God
    herding deer our way.

Someone asked *Will you two really make it?*
    I can answer only in holy numbers
hardy to northeast Ohio where our outlaw
    marriage grows even in Lent,
one crocus at a time, as we answer
    the shepherd's weathered call.

Lambing

Casting out demons at two in the morning
doesn't always work: the lamb and ewe
both died. We're sticky with blood,
barn heat, and the world's reluctance
to cooperate. Outside, fences bow
to April's blizzard, limbs
wrestle the devil. The other sheep
and their children huddle,
warming each other to sleep.

I'm selling this place for a condo:
every year, you threaten us
with a steady life.
You're awash in the blood of the lamb
as you talk of a city free
of feral cats and large vet bills.
I imagine you caged but still
pacing the fields you sold.

No, we already pay maintenance,
stripping before the cold dash
to the house where hard washing
waits with coffee.
I pick the sorrowful hay
out of your hair, one grief
at a time, and you return
the favor with talk
of the next lambing out,
Amish sales,
profitable hope for summer.
There is no escape
but bed with the valley
deep between us:
this is what we own.

Etudes for El Paso and Spanish Guitar

1973-1978

(1)
Renee borrowed a red convertible
her brother swiped from the Houston boom,
and we parked south on Scenic Drive
as dusk changed clothes for evening.

Already, her hands gave the finger
to arthritis, each joint crossed
by a surgeon, while I sat with
juvenile diabetes, too sweet for words.

We weren't even close to twenty-five,
but God was either a bitch
or absent without leave. Renee had
the smokes, I had matches,

and we set the world on fire
with wonder and pain as Juarez lights
crossed the border with all the seen
and unseen immigrants.

(2)
After the Fall, angels guard the gates
of Eden while I count forever
the lost on my desert rosary:
Glen, Joe, Mack, Miss Lolita Highball,

and others known to God
or the Centers for Disease Control.
One family hid its only son
without funeral or obituary,

without standing by the grave
in consecrated grief.
I'm told the father wrote
his child's name in the sand

each night away from the city
until he saw a ghost walker
who promised to take him, too, from the guilty earth.

(3)
Someone stuck a note on the cactus
by my apartment door
where city life met the city desert,
and my Siamese gifted me with lizards:

Bougainvillea are red,
Jacaranda are blue,
Plumeria are rotting,
So, cheating Tom, will you.

I kept this with
I love you, Thomas
another soul had written
inside my overnight bag,

and thought where my fidelities lay
before the phone rang with news
of a cousin who'd shot herself over
a wayward husband: she lived one night.

(4)
My priestly lover and I promised
New Mexico fresh Lawrencian
sins, but we were closer
to Forster's Italian sun

at the Santa Fe Opera
where we held
untranslatable passions
under an Indian blanket,

and stars kept time with the
open music. *It's like a fairy tale*
he said of each myth
as the heroine died,

but we were the ones
finding so much
and so little to sing about
between Liza Minnelli and Anita Bryant.

     (5)
When my friend Phil,
addicted to Milton and swearing
I am NOT a Catholic!
stopped his bike by a Texas road

without warning, a car knocked
him halfway to heaven:
he came down to die,
reported Renee, and he crashed

on broken knees, his behind
pointing to the God
who had it coming.
After the funeral mass

he gave his wife and children,
some of us celebrated communion
with chardonnay and Seventies' wafers:
tortilla chips, divined by a salsa indulgence.

     (6)
At the last beautification party
of the west Texas sexual revolution,
our hostess-by-the-pool explained
her new Lady Bird Johnson décor:

I brought the desert colors inside.
We approved her semi-erect bathroom taps,
the silver folds of a tissue-box vulva,
before walking into the adobe-tile

fantasy of a guest-room shower
where our five bodies broke
state laws and most commandments
before stretching on the rapturous

sunburst-orange spread,
proudly post-coital as we discussed
how water conservation is best
practiced by showering during sex.

(7)

I still hold the view from Scenic Drive.
Renee sang her poetry from a wheelchair,
I'm told, until death; one friend shares a house
with a drag queen gone Carol Channing,

another discovered the world he could lift
with weights. I cannot be faithless
although the sand blows equally
my living and my dread: Jesus

breaks my heart every day
in a new Eden that marriage
grows for us and our salvation,
and pets found on the road

to Jerusalem, Ohio. Still, some nights,
I close my eyes in God's wild mercy
to see the world all before us,
and I cross the desert again.

Personal Testimony

El Paso, 1974

No one knew anything about the Jews.
We got our money out in art,
and my mother's diamonds,
on the Swiss railway
purred the Countess that Sunday lunch
as she ignored her great-niece's flat
and the girl's boyfriend worth less
than the Texas dirt that would bury him.

Her facelift stretched between lives
in Germany and America,
and I marveled how it wiped away
history, collared by a dress that whispered
Chanel, but not *nouveau Chanel*.
The coffee she made herself
was strong enough to walk,
and she slapped her niece's hand
before serving us in sapphires
and emeralds that clutched
her polished neck with lies
dating to the eighteenth century.
But she nailed one truth that morning:
You have an accent, too.

She asked what I knew and approved
of Bartok, Chopin, before talking
rings around Wagner.
We walked across the hall
to inspect my student library
of paperback treasures.
Her sweet fingers untouched
by work traced my lips:
Someone loved you, eh?

When we left the building, she took
my arm to make me the gigolo
every Thirties movie dreamed of.
At the car, I waited for her hand,
and the guilty diamonds smiled
as she pulled me close:
Don't worry so much about God, dear one,
get to Paris and Tuscany, Florence:
You need a different sun.

Letters from the Gay Menopause House of Detention and Eternal Prayer

(1)

My right nut complains
until I collect physicians like one-nighters
from the Seventies, including
Dr. Grin and Bear It, Mr. Ducks.
who talks about manning up.
I hope his wife gives him
seventeen kinds of sexual disease,
I hope his son turns into a bigger
Julie Andrews queen than I am,
I hope his daughter's hobbies
are flannel shirts, rodeo,
and castration, I hope someday
he grins and bares his right nut
as a urologist says
It's either bacterial or cancer:
we're gonna ultrasound your balls.

(2)

Welcome to the hand-job from hell,
the *Titanic* in its iceberg.
The opposite of youth isn't age,
it's this sweet tech lubricating
each cold step as if I hadn't written
A Homo's Guide to Multiple Everything.
Did I escape AIDS and Carolina
only to listen to this kid apologize
as he kills arousal, possibly forever?
He speaks to the left one, then quiets farther west:
Your doctor will be talking to you.

(3)

Listening since I was twelve,
I cheated death thanks to insulin
and Daddy's Army latex lessons.
Now this wrecked carcass has cost me a job,
sent me back to the old one,
when, surely, what's prescribed again is Tuscany
or New Mexico: let me beauty watch the world.

Shall I dump my husband and become
a gray queen with perfect suits and a pretty
boy half my age? Those couples aren't always sad,
holding hands in museums and the better
restaurants of May through December.
Or, shall I wear the sagging life I have,
widening into welcome
and unwelcome epiphanies?

               (4)
With my shorts at my knees, I find myself
in gender equity, holding the male answer
to an ovarian cyst: what's next, a lump in my pee?
No, enough antibiotics to cure the armed forces,
The Middle-Aged Queen's Miracle Health and Beauty Regimen,
and show albums reissued on compact disks,
flying saucers from a Broadway I never knew.
This is survivor glee: I'll walk
through Rich's garden in ten thousand
pedometer steps, close enough to Eden,
sun cream streaming down
my baldness into my eyes,
orthotics lifting me toward heaven,
the diet and the dog failing to obey.
Put the Rapture on hold: I've got
a lot of falling apart to do.

Lost in the Art of Mary Cassatt

> *Your child is good for you.*
> —my mother's psychiatrist when I was four

Between her worst breakdowns,
Mama wrote my autobiography,
borrowing my I to justify
family pictures and all those
piano certificates printed in major keys.
The scrapbook emerged like a housecat
whenever Mama decided
to fatten it with my scarlet ribbons,
newspaper clippings, and all
those cards of Cassatt's madonnas
sent home to record what I'd done
that week to improve myself.

When I got too big for my own life,
Mama framed the college diplomas,
her graduate degrees in motherhood
and sanity. I took over when her fingers
began to shake, but we still edited
our story each trip home.

I've mounted the later pictures:
ailing Christmases where Daddy
raised his traditional stocking
of pennies with heavy pleasure,
Mama illuminated by the tree.
Always a good sport, she rides
her last birthday in a wheelchair,
she points to non-existent birds
we sing to. I slip in our book
a postcard from a friend:
You are exactly like your mother.

Not really. But as I write the last
caption under the obituary
with her troubled India ink,
I learn why she bothered,
why Cassatt lifted her brush:
I want to hold the mother
holding the child just a little longer.

For the Queens Who Dragged Marlene's Furs Across my Life

And draped paisley shawls around my lamps,
        so the fringe could trail into the Savannah River.
They framed Garbo and Bacall as nightstand voyeurs
        of the love that dare not violate the rules of taste
passed from Oscar Wilde to *Architectural Digest*.
        Over *drinks, luv, not cocktails,*
they confessed to meeting *Judy before booze took her voice,*
        and of course *when Rock went to Texas*
*for **Giant**, no one could keep him even then, dear,*
        out of the bars, or the cowboys.

Piling coffee table books on their lives, these sisters
        stretched shaven boys and bourbon over sofas
imported from Thirties' films. *We just returned from New York*
        meant they'd led a charge against the Christian
fellowship and bribed their bodies with nine kinds
        of penicillin. Keeping the roses as Mama wanted,
they pruned the vice squad if possible. When Ravanel
        got picked up in the park, again, two would cross
into Georgia with bail money and songs from the Broadway show
        I'd Move to Atlanta, but I Can't Leave the Folks.

I am what they blushed to be: a sixty-five-year-old southern queen
        with poodle, the love child of Liberace
and Flannery O'Connor. Walking Princess Diana
        through the rose garden, I think of the mothers
who paid for piano and dance lessons, the men
        who raised curtains, not eyebrows, over *The Nutcracker*
and let me into culture on a weekend pass. Delivered from a life
        of third-rate giggles over *him* and small town bars,
I took the trip from fear to here:
        there's no place, darlings, like home.

October in Richfield, Ohio

(note found on the kitchen counter)

Tom, the pawpaws weren't rotten—
they are ripe—
and smell and taste like banana custard.
Three halves are left over
in the fridge if you dare
to try them—just please save me
the seeds.

Ohio is Where I Hang

I love the idea of home, the South,
Aunt Marian's pound cake soaked in religious rum,
Hymn sings, hillbilly contractors moonlighting
as shade-tree mechanics, the porch fight over
whether Spanish moss is an alien or not—
Still, so many of us expats remain in Ohio.

We stay for the grace of Yankees singing
Spirituals and gospel in funereal tempos,
Their icy twangs refusing to swing low,
And enjoy the spectacle of their cooking down
Greens with too little or too much bacon
As if this delicacy were some kind of work.

We're relieved not to pass the time
With young bores talking about *Diddy's bidness,*
And the matron planning her daughter's evangelical
Wedding with the wrath of Sherman, the class of Vegas.
Boarding the plane to Cleveland, wasn't I relieved
When Tish Beauregard, already seated, turned her

Snobbish nose away though I knew
She was common and *nouveau?*
Against my will, I've found poetry in buckeyes,
Pierogies, and the button-free Amish, music
In the splatter of kitchens on Saturday nights
When Little Italies rumble Little Hungaries.

For me, now, it's the happy heartburn of a bratwurst
On Deutschland Day and Yankees answering a question
With only one word. I'll take the Greek guy roasting
A pig in his front yard and raise you two chickens
Plucked for paprikash. Ohio is my stride, so watch out:
An accordion and I are coming your way.

Gentlemen of a Certain Age Perform Your Broadway Favorites

You'll wait until five minutes after the hour,
eight if we decide to do a Judy Garland:
Will the boys go on tonight?
Refugees from thirty years
of teaching high school English and dance,
the heartbreak of public health
nursing, we wear glitter instead of medals
on our black-velvet lapels:
Jesus, four of us are even straight.
My favorite lesbian lights us
with pink-gel lies: twenty bucks
can buy a lot of salvation
and the ghost of Lawrence Welk.

Backstage, somebody warms up a voice
cracked in the rafters years ago,
another tightens his facelift
while I count the hairs lost
to Curly after too many *Oklahomas!*
We sing middle age and the child
gone to cancer, alcoholic spouses,
a law career stuck at associate drudge.
Too old now to count the house—
who cares who's out there—
we know the burden of stardom.

Cue the house lights, cue the twin pianos,
the poodles at home,
my lover gone to honey half my age.
Enter behind curtain,
sing just before it rises
to shut you the hell up,
shoulders back,
sing chins up, all of them,
two weekends only in Akron, Ohio,
the men we must be.

Poem for My Nightstand

Silence becomes you.
Thanks for not explaining why the three notches
On the bedpost don't mean what I want,
How kaleidoscopic stains came to line your drawer,
Or who carved *Thomas, I love you* on your side
Now facing the wall.

I love your antique pride:
You threw off Miss Susie's doily and the cheap
Silver lamp from Target that scarred the wall
Forever. You bear proudly the unfinished classic
Marked on page thirty-seven with a torn
Condom wrapper, a souvenir from something
Else I couldn't finish.

Of course, I want the stories
That came with you, but discretion is in the grain.
I imagine you born from a half-rotted Carolina live oak,
Salvaged and better for that redemption, styled
In the Charleston way. For the rest of our lives,
I shall lay my books and fidelity on your patient back:
A marriage of true minds, without impediment.

Queer Body

I stroll the apricot way
With a post-operative poodle
Limping to Motown therapy
And a classical music of creaks and aches:
What remains into what's left.

I am the southern queen
Your father warned you about:
A woman called the cops Tuesday
Because I sang and danced Julie Andrews
As Madam pooped on public grass—
We let the world off with a warning.

Doggie and I have matching tee shirts:
This IS straight acting.
Our scars hurt when it rains or the words
Junior High and *High School*
Return from memory like swords,
Or the buzz saw that was Daddy.

I must carry Madam up fourteen stairs now:
Three times a day, my back says
Hurt to us both.
Groaning, sighing, afraid,
Our carcasses sing of the end to come.

Until then, we live large
On and off our doctors' scales.
Her spa day costs sixty bucks a month,
I shave my own head to save twenty—
Post beauty, we dance-walk
Through the muzak of Pet World:

Why, oh why, do fools fall in love?

Coyotes Walk Up Oakdale Street on Christmas Eve

I'm a naked middle age
doing time and housework
to the beat of *Jingle Bell Rock*
when I hear neighbor Sam scream
Keep your pets inside!

There's a wildness in Ohio.
I look out my cross-boned window
to see three coyotes strolling
through our seductive lights,
ready to eat what Santa brings.

Maybe they'd want to gnaw my belly
down from a barrel to a six-pack,
or feast on my poodle, Madam Princess,
who barks insanely
from her plush sofa-throne.

I can't help but like their loping,
the natural rhythm of free beasts.
I got close, once, in north Texas
and saw their eyes deep and wide
as my grandmother's when she said

I left home to save my mind.
That may be the story
of these coyotes, too.
We're all trying to save something
in Ohio from the cold and politics.

The coyotes turn the corner now,
and my prayers wish them luck.
I go back to the dust rags
and *It's Beginning to Look a Lot Like Christmas.*
The phone rings with someone's panic,

but I keep cleaning up the past.
This afternoon, behind my mop,
I'll walk with three coyotes
to some wild stable where
we'll bring what gifts we have.

Daddy Fishing Alone at Whittle's Pond

The nervy frogs on lily pads
Wait to pick off breakfast;
The odd twang of a fiddle string
As a varmint hides under green water;
The off-key silence of being left alone—

No need now to try to read words
Jumbled as worms and taxes:
This is the prewar peace
Of a day's fishing and cleaning fish,
A rapture of hymns
And popping beer cans because

Trout bite best that way.
Good to leave his sissy-boy-son
Home with his whining about the heat,
Mud, and fish-hooks.
Good to have the wife gone with her
Shock treatment and telling him

What he's thinking as if she knew.
He's an army man once more,
Or a Florida boy unafraid
Of a world bordered by the turpentine mill
And Deakel Cemetery where his sister named
Alpha Omega rests in death too soon.

Let the skillet spit as hush puppies
Fall in like friends. *Here, Twilight,*
he shouts, and the dog comes,
leading just for him
every blessed star.

TWO

"Do you still say your prayers?"
—my mother, Sam Ella Hair Dukes, from her bedroom to me in mine, sometime in the late 1990s

Camp Meeting

Jesus was best served with catfish
and hush puppies deluxe:
chopped onion, green pepper, and deep fat
hallelujahs! got us in the spirit

by Whittle's Pond. I worshipped
green-bean casseroles, with Aunt Edna's fluff
on the side. We brought Mama's
Bad Baby Squash Bake

the doctors preach against,
and yesterday's fried chicken, cold,
because it tastes better that way,
Aunt Ruby said, like revenge

and the idea of marrying the one
you love. Our hymn sing
made some possums run
right through the doings:

when the men laughed too much,
Preacher stopped
the ruckus with
Let us pray

and we thanked the Lord
for everything in the tarnation
that Aunt Ruby called
holy goddam hell.

Even as a boy holding paper plates
doubled to support my faith,
I knew I'd fly away soon
with my wicked gluttony:

still, with Mama crying over sins
she didn't commit, and Daddy
full of the Old Testament,
I loved this communion,
knowing God and I had
the whole world
in our hands.

Hawk in December

This is the man my father dreamed
of being: in charge of wild tress,

beautiful even cold, small things
below made smaller and afraid.

Daddy cursed what he could not
grasp; when lupus shook

his barber-hands, he cried
about lost customers,

my failings as a man,
the fish we didn't catch.

Still, he never gave me a gun:
Them is mean things, boy.

When I flew to Texas
For those young years of college

tequila, he spread wide
his stories of Fort Bliss

soldiering; we curved
our lives close to the sun

that, forever, throws
the hawk's shadow

on the wary earth.

Gospels from the Lower Shelf

                (1)
When Mama got her mind plugged in and cleaned
        every five years or so,
           Aunt Ruby would pick me up after school
           in her Nova: *I love my sister, but this is bullshit.*

We'd go to Cody's Bar-b-Que for redneck pork
        and *Jesus ain't lookin'* onion rings,
           along with Carolina cole slaw to avoid getting
        the trots or packed in. I'd have two

of Daddy's tip quarters for the juke box
        so Aunt Ruby could get the vinyl booth blues:
        yes, it was *Cryin' Time* again.
        When I was fifteen, Aunt Ruby said to me

in front of God and the Men's Methodist Prayer Group:
        Always use a rubber and you'll never be sorry.
        Back home, when we couldn't bear to open the car door
        to face life, we'd split a stick of Juicy Fruit

and diddle with the dial until we found the song that meant
        Lord help my Christ, I don't know, I just don't know.

                (2)
Mama was not always In; mostly, she was Out.
        We'd lie head to foot and foot to head
        on her bed and gossip about sane people
        until Aunt Ruby stopped by, fresh from Sunday worship:

Dolly and Buster shared a beach house each year with the Millers.
        The Millers had a son, and of course Dolly and Buster
        had Wanda Kaye. One night, the big folks drove to Charleston
        for dinner, leaving the kids behind for pizza and television.

Now, because Dolly has spent half her life with her head
        up her twat, she forgot her purse. When they got back
        to the house, Dolly hollered WANDY KAYE, HELP ME
        FIND MY PURSE. Of course, at that moment, the Miller boy's

Thing was in Wanda Kaye's purse, if you get my meaning.
        When Wanda Kaye heard her mother's voice,
        her purse clamped like a vise around the boy's Thing.
        Child, you couldn't GIVE me Hilton Head for the confusion

that night. They had to dope Wanda Kaye to get the Miller boy
        Out, and they had to dope Dolly to get her off the Miller kid
        Aunt Ruby fixed me in the crosshairs of her Army green eyes:
        Child, don't you ever get into a tight like that!

        (3)
Reading to children at the Home
        was my *Project for a Better World*
        required of students considered for Honors.
        Aunt Ruby swore her job there putrified her soul

but she drove me until I got my license.
        This is Purgatory, I wrote: everyone waited
        for the Second Coming or the next shift.
        Not one of those kids understood what I read:

As Aunt Ruby said, *Sometimes God goes out for a smoke.*
        She played the ponies at Northfield Park on her breaks,
        and six volunteers invited me to join their tap class.
        Once after I worked Sunday midnight to eight

for extra points, Aunt Ruby drove me to breakfast and sang
        spirituals that carried to all the places I've never been.
        In an alto that locked the gates to hell, she declared for us all
        I'm satisfied with Jesus, and he's satisfied with me.

(4)

May is Mental Health Month
        is how I answered the Honors English Essay Question
        about irony in everyday life. Such attitude was
        Not Appreciated, and I got demoted to Regular Track
On the same day Aunt Ruby and I took Mama to Psych Admitting
        for-the-last-time-please-God. The tech didn't
        believe we lived at the corner of Sanitarium Drive
        and Faith Lane until Aunt Ruby sassed his face:

And who put this looney bin on Infirmary Road?
        Finally, they wheeled Mama past, crying, crying
        as she always did at such times,
        like those weeping Madonnas on the barns in Barberton.

Back home, too tired to breathe almost,
        I put Patsy Cline on the old turntable and let her sing
        through the window screens. Aunt Ruby and I rode
        our past on the slow porch glider that keeps

every secret, tucked under a quilt too tatty now
        for anyone but family, while the stars called us
        baby, baby all night long.

Idol Worship

Summer camp decrees against graven images
meant nothing to the bodies of Baptist youth.
New boy body hair, the surprise
of breasts, everything erect as the chapel roofs cross.

Each morning, we dragged puberty to prayers
before breakfast segregated by sex;
each evening, fresh from swimming in stolen glances,
we wondered if anybody necked in the China missions.

Counselors scored muscles on both sides of the net,
sprang from the high dive in arcs of sexual promise,
and slid visible jock straps and sports bras into home plate.
Dropping sweat and underwear in the showers,

young men confessed their hairy bodies skipped college chapel
for the fellowship of girls named *Cyn* smuggled into dorms.
We boys on the brink dreamed all night of panties
on doorknobs warning off intruders, then washed

our sheets next morning before Brother Waters
told us he didn't crack the whip about masturbation:
we had to tell the Wagener boys that meant *jerking off*.
Each day our personal relationship with Jesus Christ

took a hit. Brenda slipped her top down in the lake
for fifteen seconds: Junior said they looked like little frogs.
Carl puked at the sight, then told,
so all three had to stand at dinner to pray.

Our parents came the last day for final altar call,
but everyone had been saved at least once
to all six verses of *Just as I Am*.
As baptized Eros trudged to Fords and Chevies,

we heard counselors run screaming to the lake:
the Word made flesh indeed.
The way of the cross led home, all right,
but inside we swam forever beneath the naked sun.

Abiding Light

Members who got themselves shot at church
for the directory received a discount on prints,
and we saved whatever we could, money or souls.
My dress pants itched as if they knew
one Sunday soon I would throw them
out of the closet and refuse to go.
Mama wore Pentecostal red, Daddy his men's store suit
with black dress shoes and the white socks
that made me want to die on his behalf.
In the Ford Falcon, we sat like twentieth century art:
Baptist Primitive.

I saw the pale band of divorce circling
the photographer's finger as he tried
to comb over his misery. But he made us
laugh when we saw the light at his command
in the only portrait of us, together.

Nobody paid no never-mind six weeks later
to the shadows behind Mama and Daddy.
With one breakdown to her credit,
 two to go, Mama tithed her best Baptist smile
  in spite of faculty meetings and lessons
 that buckled the heart.
Daddy grinned through dyslexia
that sentenced him to cutting hair
until lupus shook his hands into the grave.
And I? A shy upturning
above and behind my parents,
original sins lurking in the genes,
bad blood from his, diabetes from hers,
soon to wipe that smile off my face.

But here we rest still, on my bedroom wall,
always asking God to lay us down to sleep,
our souls to keep, faded and fading.
We are, of course, in *love.*

Mrs. Bendremer

Judy had a shoebox of pictures,
and she invited them and me to tea
after gardening.

She didn't introduce her family
to just anybody: Aunt Heidi, Cousin Gretl,
Uncle Who? some Rachels, Abes, Davids,
and all the so many.

Folks under happy trees,
at table, bar mitzvahs,
the scowls of grown sisters standing
too close to each other,
some brothers in hard business,
brides and grooms, all kosher.

Judy got out:
I remember running down a street
in Vienna: we had to run.
I was five, in new shoes,
fancy little girl shoes with bows,
and one bow fell off, but Papa picked
it up in the street even with his boxes
and the luggage. Mama put it
back on in the train, and I knew
then we would be all right.

That first tea, I asked about the picture people:
All gone, mein geld, all perished.
Now I wonder about the pictures: Judy's dead,
the house cleaned out, no one left who remembers—
Did those people burn a second time?

Odella, at Eighty

They say that nouns are the first to go.
After teaching English for decades,
I search the lexicon to make
natural the unnatural order of things:
We just lost Edward, our older son.

I'm retired from nothing:
Shall I deal my vocabulary flashcards
as memento mori, with *faith* and *grace*
trumping *grief*? Explicate irony
in the phrase *from cradle to grave*?
These questions everyone fails:
I gave no such tests,
I am kinder than God.

On her deathbed, my friend Sam Ella said
The Lord is merciful.
Maybe, but I wish he had better manners.
I refuse to become the myths I taught,
Hecuba wailing about the dead of Troy
or Mother Courage with too much to say.
I'm weary of epiphanies and redemption,
those promises meant to repair what's left.

This weekend, I'll walk Pawley's Island beach
with Edward's granddaughters.
They'll fly with the gulls, bully the surf,
while I, earthbound, pick up shells,
listening to voices without words:
We will not perch on the soul.

Son, Watermelon Should Be Blood Red

We mean-spat the seeds to the ground
Because Daddy lived by anger
And wanted to hit the world and me,
But Mama told him *Watch it, Sergeant John.*

Sometimes we swallowed the seeds
To prove we were men,
Or gulped cherry pits:
Being peculiar was his revenge,

But people only stared
When he bisected melons
With a sugar cane blade,
Sharp and deadly as he felt—

I blushed for us all—
Or when he dug out melon chunks
As if they were muscle
With the same Army knife

He used to clean bass
And fix a hundred manly things.
Sometimes I bled juice all over
My white Baptist shirt:

Stand up straight, goddamit:
Cain't you do anything right?
You don't know nothin',
Not a fuckin' thing that matters.

Grown enough later to be armed
With a spoon, I lifted melon miniatures
To my lips, clearing the palate
In a room of silver and the bourgeoisie.

When I dropped a melon piece
On her lace, our hostess, too kind,
Placed her ruby fingers on my hand:
Are you all right, dear?

Education

Zygote to stillbirth in nine successive jars:
What a little family!
Welcome to the Augusta Museum,
Second floor, East: *Life Sciences.*

At ten, I wanted to take home the last,
A baby boy with red hair.
He leaned forward in his jar,
Eyelashes curled in an amniotic fluid

Of formaldehyde, forever waiting.
Surely he could live if I willed him to,
A pet baby brother.
Cousin Lou Lee started to cry

Country mouse tears, but the old guide
Raised his eyebrow wings:
Vat?! Don' dey teach you nosszing?
Zis is part of life, little gull.

His bowtie shrugged common sense.
We stood before dispassion,
Mama smiling her teacher's smile
Of victory through truth.

I tried to find a chapter in *Your Own Mysteries*
About the jar boy, but he wasn't there.
I'm sure he's long gone,
Sparing the squeamish and fearful,

But he did his job: though I've walked
Through valleys of syringes and insulin
And blood loss, I fear no post-operative fact,
Never met the devil of self-pity.

You are an outlier, says the doc
Fifty years on: I live in the kingdom
Of the haunted and the grateful,
Keeping my ghosts in line.

Stealing Lumber on a Sunday Afternoon

(for Rick Bragg)

Lucas hauls a devil's load of pine
in his daddy's pick-up
that the law loves to hate:
welcome to Alabama.
He contracts for every poor white
whose mama picked hours
of someone else's cotton and tomatoes
to feed her kids with, whatever
Big Man said she could tote home.

Let Methodists take the high road to Jesus:
Lucas rocks his axle on clay so rutted
the sheriff can't follow.
He's got 190,000 miles on this life
where *rehab* means the rich
are messing in your business again.

Once he shot the mayor's mule dead
on general principles and won
fifty dollars from Jubal Slade,
now doing time for statutory rape
of all the sugar named *Georgia* he could find.
Lucas himself got eighteen months
for a wrong turn that took
his illegal hooch to a debutante picnic:
it pleasured him to hear the blazer boys
scream like girls.

Azaleas bloom as he passes,
wild dogwood take a bow.
He'll buy his grandpa some Red Chief,
his sister coffee and steak,
yellow roses for their mama's grave:
Eastertime's a-comin',
Lucas sings, *for ever'body.*

Barrier Island Lullaby for 3 a.m.

South of Charleston, the blues build
strong bones in joints
boiling with gullah stew
and women in halter tops
who electrify guitars between smokes
and the Georgia line.

Son, this is education
Daddy said the night Conway Poole
sliced his brother over a Wal-Mart tart
and a bag of grass that would
inform his next gospel album
dedicated to whatever pieces of Junior
that Conway and the Lord
left walking around.

Here in Low Country
we all record for the Hellbound label:
when the Rapture comes
with early Elvis, I'll be upstairs
getting laid by a one-way ticket
to the free clinic and dreams
of Carolina boys who slick back
the cops with Dee-Lux Grease
and some mean Saturday night stride.

Tonight, though, I'll let Jesus
sing bass for my hard-case songs
doing time in or out of the pen.
Savannah's just a few shacks away;
when the rhythm's right,
I'll hitchhike to some sugar
and check salvation at the door
where my baby's name is always bad news.

Try Me

James Brown called Aunt Ruby
every bad-woman word
he knew that smelly morning
she processed his courthouse intake:
he'd crossed mean and drunk
over the Georgia-Carolina line
of our Baptist peaches,
sweet lynchings of prosperity.

Later, one night,
Aunt Ruby and I drove
by the juke joint she operated
with sorry-assed I. P. Poole—
Lord, how she cussed James Brown's
soul when the radio sang *Try Me,*
but we rolled the windows
honeysuckle down to fall
in love, again, with longing
and loneliness so bad that we split

a Diet Rite to the tune of stories
about her rotten men and mine
all the way to Heaven's Here
Barbeque in Columbia,
where we ate so much
funky pork we almost turned
common before promising
each other not to get the heartbreak again,

much less anything *private,*
no matter what bad news
we kissed on Saturday nights
when James Brown brought home
the forever God Almighty
pine-tree blues.

My Buddy

In line, someone whispers
Cremation has taken place,
the obituary given voice.
I am like a crazy uncle,
expected and dreaded:
I am the familiar of this family.

Kyle was fifteen,
all freckles and honesty,
lost to *dying in bed syndrome*
where the sleeping diabetic's
blood sugar drops so low
the brain starves.
I taught him how to inject
oranges with insulin,
then himself. I am old
with this disease now older
than four decades inside me,
killing grace.

Kyle, you can live forever with this.
He gave me handmade birthday cards,
said I was his bestest best buddy.

In front of Mary and Walt,
I murmur the Baptist pleasantries
of my childhood, religion
with religion removed.
Mary hugs me; Walt starts to cry
because he knows I know
what he's thinking.
Yes, Walt, why couldn't
it have been me?

The receiving line spits me out
for a cup of coffee plus perfumed
conversation with old friends
and every flower Holland could export.
We try to last a decent interval
but run to our cars a bit too soon
as others take up the slacking grief.

I live in the selfishness of survival,
but, kid, I would have saved you
if I could—I would save them all.

Walking the Moon at 3 a.m.

> *even the darkness is not dark to you;*
> *the night is bright as the day,*
> *for darkness is as light to you.*
>   Psalm 139:12

The dog is full and so am I,
her petulant lover,
so we head outside
to the pink champagne
and smoke of February, Ohio.

Madam pulls us toward the best
pissing snow as the horses next door
purr in stalled satisfaction.
Leashed to duty,
we own the cold world:
she sniffs crocuses
hibernating in lust.
I whisper *Mama, Daddy,*
I conjure Aunt Ruby's full-moon
snuff biscuits always served
beside family secrets.

Soon Madam gets religion
about ice, and tugs
us toward the door.
I don't mind
our silent turn:
this Baptist winter
redeems us
with what's below ground
and will rise again.

THREE

"You're in charge, you know."
    —Dr. Henry Langston, our family doctor, when I was diagnosed with Type 1 diabetes in September 1972

Genuine Antics for Sale

Sign on the highway near White Pond, South Carolina

Driving in Ohio past and present,
I recall the poultry wholesaler's boast
Biggest Breasts Around
and his scary *Cocks Half Off*.
Radio going at the farmers' market,
a Mennonite asks us to
Jam with Our Jelly.
while another straw hat promises
Bread Big as Your Mother's Behind
with an invitation to
Taste my Daughter's Honey.

The holy comes easily to the Midwest:
One True God, Turn Left,
Then Three Miles Ever Sunday
and *Virgin Mary on the Barn*
Twice Daily 2:00 and 6:00
Bring Rosary for Ten Dollar Blessing.
Indiana once invited me to
Dip into Our Holy Waiters
with the reminder that
Jesus Can Touch You Everywhere.

Travel has its own rewards:
We crossed Jordan, Ontario, to see
Texas Barbeque
made by all those Canada cowboys
in honor of Founder's Day,
plus their *Real Kentucky Bluegrass.*
All this south of *Balls Falls*
and the orchard keeper's charge
Take Some Fruits Home With You,
a command I'm too old for now,
but in my day . . . .

With each mile now,
Closed for the Season
means mostly the wrong things,
and I know that *Rough Road Ahead*
is God's Truth. Still, I look
for those signs and wonders
written for the almost blind,
and I see, and see again.

Guys with Their Hands in Their Pockets

Mansfield, Ohio

Carl Lee and his buddies stand like trees
listening to the pick-up engine idle
as they idle on Sunday afternoon:
no Steelers, or maybe the women
ran them out of the triple-wides
and the houses Paw-paw built himself
with black lung.

As if he'd found love for the first time,
L. W. leans his hard-case body
over the motor. Hank and Lucas
wait for the law and child support warrants
coming Monday, although the Honda plant
laid off Jesus Christ and everybody else.
Carl Lee would tell the law
laid off means you can't get
our own grits, let alone baby formula,
but he knows no law listens to him.

The others *Yeah* and *Good job, you cuss.*
L.W. nods with the country cool
of a man who beat up an honors kid
senior year and did time for it.
The others shuffle in Meemaw's raked dirt:
maybe they'll sniff out a six pack, smokes,
and a trio of bored Wandas, or Merle
will haul up with a notion.

But as they wait for the world to crank,
Carl Lee slips away like a possum
to listen for a dog barking,
a train, some church organ left to hum,
anything with a heart, singing.

A Woman Bathes in the Ohio River on Sunday Afternoon

I put up my hair.
I lower my colors:
a white blouse of surrender,
black pants of mourning.

My daughter, the eldest,
made this body
of full breasts,
global belly,
thighs that can crush cars.
My stretch marks stretch
from pregnancy
to her funeral last month.

Now, my husband passes
cars on midnight runs
that will not kill him.
My son in Seattle drinks cool
coffee but calls home every day
to scare off bad things.
My Paris son cried so hard
his girlfriend offered to marry him.

The water raises me
above the nonsense of suicide.
I bob, a post-menopausal cork.
Some boys on the bank
snicker at my nipples,
a woman says
John, call the cops, it's indecent.
Bury your child, lady,
if you want indecent.

The summer she turned thirteen,
I paid my daughter twenty dollars
to teach me to swim:
now you won't drown, Mom.
Today, the sun's rod and staff
comfort me. Perhaps
I shall take up knitting,
or the ponies, or song styling
in better lounges.

Until then, I am art:
Still Life with Floating Mother.
I know how to get
to shore.

Red Onions

They put any day on its feet.
Yes, the old calico complains
When I slice into one:

Mad juices seem to sting
Everything.
Always use the sharpest knife,

Mama said: this year,
August is the sharpest knife,
With the dog's surgery

And autumn already
Crunching its way toward us.
I make do with the leftovers

Of divorce: dull blades,
The cutting board so old
A friend won't come
Into my kitchen any more.

Don't make the slices too thin
Holler all the women who raised me.
I zigzag through the hard surface

To the heart of what matters,
Sharp, enough to share.
Not to cry would be cheating,

My ghosts proclaim:
I need this Old Testament fruit,
The peculiar charity of its taste.

Ohio Farm Boy

No barn is pretty if you're the one
who painted it. Blistered brushes,
cracked Amish and Mennonites
knowing Jesus and cow jokes,
Dad who paid us all by the hour
in sandwich bags of change.

Get a job that don't depend on the weather
he said one summer when the boards
and our hands split open in the cornball
heat. We drew buzzards, we smelled
so bad, and cows under trees looked
at stupid us crinkling in the sun.

Tourists made us quaint against
our will. In the store, wearing an Amish
hat, I told one lady that if she took
my picture, *I'll marry your daughter
and eat her pussy*. Mr. Cowan just
laughed and gave me a free orange soda.

Too tired to sleep, I'd read the night
away. Paint odors came through the window
like ghosts, and nightlife sang
prayers for rain and its sweet power
to delay this world of work and salt:
but next morning, we got on with it,
and on with it.

Ruth Speaks After the Buckeye Jewish Center Adult Tap Class

To the beat of middle-age,
my fat rolls in natural rhythm
as I atone for the gluttonous
high holy days by turning
exercise into art and praying
that my children won't call,
while praying that they do.
Outside, the world is all
apple floors and ginger skies,
but here I spring into step.

I see you, Tom, watch us
as we Rubber City broads
shake our booty.
What I've got belongs
to Sir Isaac Newton,
the bastard, but I dance
all over gravity,
a benefit performance
for my benefit.

That's what I tell Walter,
who's saved all his life
and never lived.
He'll die to make me
rich while I'm cruising
the Ann Miller fantasy line.
I've buried a son, I've got
a Holocaust museum in a gift box
of my mother's pictures turning to ash,
I've got sixty pounds that need
another home. And more lessons
to learn, too: when the Messiah comes,
I'll do what he does,
backwards and in high heels.

Baptists in Oberlin

Hang a right where metaphors protest
   the war, and you'll find them at the corner
   of East College and Jericho Road,
   still dressed in stained glass.
   Afflicted with salvation,
   they lay hands on *Wage Peace* buttons
   and take the first plate offering

a stone's throw from abolitionist judgment.
   They pray that Eddie will return to the path
   of Prozac and the art department,
   they pray as Estelle and her white Rapunzel braid
   lift Joe's aching back to the Lord,
   they forgive the demon-possessed government.
   With horns and a lap organ,
   they seek the gift of sense for language poets,
   that all may find gender-neutral words
   for God who, surely, before the Rapture will bring

cushions for the pews. Now comes the second round
   for the progressive quarter, the wayward penny,
   to serve this week's special mission: a garden
   for the poor in spirit and tomatoes.
   I join the altar call for my Mama's cucumbers,
   Daddy's squash plants with leaves big
   as the elephant ears of Saturday morning
   Tarzan movies where Johnny Weissmuller
   swang through Eden in the way of all hot flesh.

I return from Africa for full immersion
   in today's sermon: *Are Your Dreams Too Small?*
   Yes, always the guilty *yes,* so I'll tithe bigger
   brownies for fellowship, forgive Unitarians
   their tedium, then sing *Hallelujah!* to the man
   who brings his dog, keeping faith one beagle at a time.

Miss Cleveland Drag 1979 Packs Away Liza Forever

My Liza gave me the prize, too long ago.
I should have won the year before,
with Barbra, but the judges
went with Miss Thing's Diana Ross
to show they were liberal—and Thing
wasn't even Black: I'm told she'd baked
in her Daddy's barbeque sauce.
Want to guess where we exiled
that Thing the year I won? Can you
say *Outhouse, West Virginia?*

If only Jake were here to help.
But of course he couldn't stay
out of Edgewater Park,
and the bikers couldn't stay out of him,
so he got cursed with AIDS. The best
of my husbands, he gave me
every lilac boa I have.
We scattered his ashes in Lake Erie,
but a wind blew him in my eyes
and I've been teary ever since.

Yes, yes, I hear the studs downstairs
that Terry sent over: young, dumb, and full
of minimum wage plus what they hustle
on the side. I want to send them back
to the Fifties' melodrama they fell from,
but a girl has to have cash, especially
a queen of a certain age like me.

Let the moving boys wait
as I soak in Liza's beads
and spangles one more time
before wrapping my soul in mauve
muslin for somebody else.
I'll haul these boxes myself down three flights,
but don't worry about me, dears:
life is a lot more than a cabaret,
and I'm man enough for the job.

I Need from You an Advisement

I'll be Christian about her later,
but right now, she's a volcano
in striped pants and cocktail top,
ready to blow. Her dirty feet
with red toenails squidget in sandals
worn flatter than Miss Grundy's chest
as she bends for her crumpled transcript.

Her inner beauty threatens to spill out
her bra top, but it's the back crack—
I see London, I see France,
I see your purple thong.
She chirps about her two-point-three
grade point and coaching
central Ohio to greatness
with something called *gifted education.*
We assault the Dean's office twice, thrice,
with her questions about avoiding
as many credits as possible.
She writes it all down with a lavender pen
whose feather salutes each word
with a wave.

Oh, Lord, I need advisement myself.
It's the end of the day,
the end of my life,
when she assures me,
for no reason at all,
I'm not a femi-Nazi.
I want to say, *Child, I believe you,*
I know what you are, I know
what I am, too.

I am a man who got three degrees,
who's paid to pump sunshine up your bum,
as my Australian colleague says.
Tomorrow, I'll feel bad
about these open admissions,
tomorrow, I'll feel guilt, maybe,
about class, though my own daddy
was a pig farmer,
but right now, child, as you leave
I know only one thing:
We both need a bath.

January in the Ohio River Valley

Not for me those lines longing for spring:
I'll take storm-bound relatives, the heart-broken glass jars
of summer tomatoes floating in the basement,
my daughter's middle-school snowman blessed
with a naughty carrot and Christmas oranges for breasts.
She reads in the hall as the principal blushes
over her transgendered art, all of us gloved
because the heat called in sick

Lives slide on ice for six months
and debate the amount of salt required to save a marriage.
We're nowhere near Cincinnati clubs
hot with Republican lust for museum nudes,
not even close to the college bars of Columbus
where cool doesn't mean your spouse's fingers
in your pants after two hours of conjugal snow
shoveling that threaten afternoon sex: *I think it froze off*

South of Coshocton, New Philly, of everything,
we'll be gosh-darned about the forecast and flirt
with anyone who ploughs us to freedom
on school days. Seduced by mail-order,
we pout until bedtime removes
our cataloged layers of down and flannel,
courtly lovers at seventeen degrees. Snow sparks
a quarter moon: tonight, winter frees the body best.

Many Bright Mansions Above

Volunteering the midnight-to-eight,
I hold the half-brained baby
for the mother who cannot bear
what she has borne,
the father who smokes
his own soul outside,
ignoring the signs
trying to forbid grief
from catching fire.

The preemie ICU nurses
crack the skies a bit,
so the baby with no mind
and I can hear Ohio
geese announce
We fly at dawn.
I answer first with
Brahms' lullaby
but that bores everything,
so I switch to Mama's spirituals,
praying blues.

With 3 a.m. coffee,
I sing this child across
the Jordan into many
bright mansions above
where Aunt Ruby tells God
You orta know better,
and my parents set the baby
in a dresser-drawer manger
with a Favorite Story quilt:
that's all they had
to save me, and it worked.

FOUR

"Yes, she thought, laying down her brush in extreme fatigue,
I have had my vision."
—Virginia Woolf, *To the Lighthouse*

Goose Up a Tree at Beaver Marsh

We all know how she feels:
You aim for the heavens
only to find yourself at dusk
stuck on a dead tree
so stubborn it can't fall down.
No wonder she's honking mad.

Remember, we don't mate for life
goes the gander, while close by
two herons pose as if their blue
feathers are the new black.
A turtle older than melancholy,
larger than a bishop,
surfaces long enough to show
off his star-bruised shell.

I cross the wooden bridge,
marking my life in pedometer steps
as a beaver splashes hard
in the creek to get away
from it all.

He can't, of course,
any more than the goose
or the fifty deer who starve
each winter here in the park
meant to save them.

Yet, we walk in the valley
of the shadow of Akron, Ohio,
trying to escape, always,
but caught in the mystery of flight.

Knives

They are private things.
Slicing vegetables this Amish morning,
safe in the work no one wants,
I thank the zucchini for its willingness
to yield, the profligate tomatoes, and six
stubborn onions crying before the blade.

The radio mourns our new country dead
as my paring knife circles the globes
of oranges, kiwi, and pears.
I will offer grief some ambrosia
from these hours of apples
and cherries who require the smallest sword.

Not all sharp labor is sweet: knives know
hard Christmas twine, the mean coins
of fish scales, how to bleed a hen that's past setting.
In a few hours, they will carve this holiday
and cut the cake before I clean
them in American sorrow once again.

A Mary Cassatt Suite

after paintings and a drawing in the Allen Memorial Art Museum

Feeding the Ducks

Ducks are the least of it.
The women in pastels
Show the child how to offer
Her hand to the wildness
Out there, how to trust
The unknown that wants
Her gifts.

The women in color
Show the girl how to cast
Her bread upon the waters,
Take wanton risk
Of gifts thrown to the needy
World.

The women guard the girl
Standing in a boat
As she learns to rock
Her life between work
And the sweet, fat arms
That will never let
Her drown.

Margot Wearing a Bonnet

Clothes bring such responsibility
to children, no matter how young
or beautifully named.
She knows the burden of color,
the candor of display: she does not
dimple or condescend
to anyone, herself least of all.

Her art is in her eyes
that show the bonnet,
frames her desire to know
everything at once.
She owns the face
of a good student not above
talking back.

She isn't happy enough
for the moment, or ready
to be an artist's model.
That bonnet faces front
but she looks to the right:
what does she hear?

Sketch of Elsie's Head

She's hardly there,
an imagined child
given the barest outlines
of a life.

She's caught between
two sketchy lumps—
of women or mountains,
who knows.

Yet she's startled
by what
she sees,
we share her surprise
and turn to look

for the ghosts.
We can't see
the hauntings,
fingers reaching
for a throat,
the knife ready
to cut a ruby necklace
or a vein:

Too bad for us.
Too bad for Elsie.

Beagle

A stray, of course, and haunting me still:
All pink kerchief and collar, afraid
Behind the hurricane fence in some trees.

Someone dumped her like a girlfriend
On the public golf course, I bet.
For a day-and-a-half, she

Hid from the fallen world,
Peeking from behind an oak.
I tossed food and biscuits

And other useless good intentions
Her way: Animal Rescue
Snarled it would get to her

When they could.
Then she was gone
To mystery or death or an attempt

To cross the road to salvation.
I failed her.
I failed so many who looked my way.

I cannot solve the problems,
I cannot solve the problems.

The Only Time I Wished I Were Straight

> *"Son, always tell the unvarnished truth"*
> —Daddy to me on the front stoop

The only time I wished I were straight
was that Christmas at Bloomingdale's
when the tall girl, almost blonde, prettier
than any pre-Raphaelite cliché,
stood behind the glass counter
as I looked at ties.

I liked the Republican one,
all stripes and blue purpose.
She laughed and drew the tie
from its nest with slender fingers.
We stood there in a flirtatious glow,
and I smiled in a way
we both misunderstood.

Wrong about us, too, an older clerk
took my credit card and the tie to the register,
so the girl and I could get together.
I wanted to be the boy
who would explain he was in town
interviewing and maybe we could meet
for a drink when she got off.

We'd go to dinner in Chinatown that night,
and someplace poor the next and the next.
I'd fly back from lousy Indiana
every three weekends on grad school money,
and she would say how she was sick of New York.
We'd get married that June
because I'd landed this job,
and we were perfect for each other,
although everyone agreed it was too soon.

I walked out of Bloomies with that tie and that dream,
sorry to do the right thing for us both.
I hope she didn't settle for a jerk
or date the dreck that some women date.
I lost the tie about five years later in Chicago.
A weekend fling packed it accidentally on purpose
because he knew I wanted to be there
with another man who didn't want to sleep with me.
I bought a tie that afternoon at Marshall Field's
from a twinkie I needed to bitch-slap
even harder than he deserved.

As I walked back to the hotel,
I thought of the Bloomingdale girl
as I do every Christmas. Even now:
fat, bald, older than a dream,
I want to be Prince Charming,
for us both.

Marriage Blanc

Each time Mike leaves
after the summer weekend,
I spend the night
or two or three or four
in the unwashed sheets of the guest bed,
as if Mike and I were married,
or had been frantic lovers
and were still.

I dream
not of Mike's two or three serious
boyfriends, beautiful music
long gone, or the time
I slept with Mr. Irish Cologne,
then realized the guy,
who talked too much for 1984,
was sleeping with Mike, too.

I carry
our dream marriage inside,
where Mike color-coordinates
the cat with the rugs,
as I explain to the style section
why our dinner parties are
always on the home tour of better lives.

Finally, on, say, Thursday
I wash and dry this fantasy
on *extra gentle*,
then iron the linens
to my will. I make
the bed we'll lie in,
happily ever after.

New Thinking on How to Protect the Heart

(title of a story in *The New York Times*)

(for Lyra)

In the parking lot of Akron Family Restaurant,
a woman with white hair
held a deep-and-wide umbrella
over a girl.

The girl leaned a bit and clutched
the woman's free arm:
the rain confused her walking.
She stumbled twice, not badly.
She wore a spring-green raincoat.

As I pulled the heavy glass door open,
I saw that the girl had Down Syndrome
and lousy vision.

Yet, someone had made up her blue eyes
with the wisdom of a fine mascara
and gave her face foundation and blush,
but not too much.
The dress cared about the girl who wore it;
her shoes were first cousin to Mary Janes,
with a strap across the lower ankle.
She wore her hair the way you wish
your sister wore hers.

As they passed, the woman said
Thank you
and the girl smiled
Easter
and the day was
Easter! Easter! Easter!
until the sun went down.

The Sewing Circle and Altar Guild of
of St. Michael's Episcopal Church

Handmaidens to the Lord, my foot:
God follows them.

They reject the ancient whines of saints,
Mary's bleeding heart;

You'll find them Tuesday mornings,
Some Fridays, or At Home,

Needling complacent threads and demons,
Making crochet out of chaos.

When you've buried a husband or two,
A favored child, that sophomore year,

The world holds no surprises:
Why not become miraculous?

No sister-at-the-church-door goes without
A baby blanket, a sweater, a meal,

And a sharp talking to about her life.
No sugar in this tea, my dear,

From women who still say *my dear,*
Stand tall for Jesus, and expect the same from you.

Saturdays, they clip thorns, scraggly greens, and irony
From altar roses and mums:

These women care about everything,
Know the right stitch can vanquish despair.

They are the substance we hope for,
Evidence of the unseen, seen.

Before the Rapture Comes

Let's not underrate gentlemen of a certain age,
Sleeping nude.

So what if youth expanded into bellies
That make us sing *Climb Every Mountain,*

Or the wrinkles of wrinkles refuse
To relax even at three a.m.?

Never mind that some men now require
Deforestation by clippers while others believe

Atonal means their sad, slack muscles.
No one in these beds will cheat death,

And we know it. Better to explore
Old bodies with spotted hands,

Up hill and down dale, that rue
What was and will be lost.

Here's to chicken legs and bald pates,
Old man snores that scare the deaf,

Bodies of experience waiting
In faith and dreamy desire.

Brandywine Falls in June

We wade on azure pebbles,
We wear our trousers rolled:

Even turtles trust you here.
You ration that smile like a secret:

The ghosts of Garbo and Tallulah swoon.
What a man you are in this light:

I hear the crackling jealousy of saints.
Keep me close to the madness

Of the plaid in your summer shirt,
Your crying *help! help!* in our sleep.

How you rile the homesteading geese,
And answer the woodpecker's knock:

Who's there? We're not buying!
Your blue-eyed mischief will never die,

Nor your wild infidelities with pretty boys
From eighteen to eighty:

Give me the sweet sting
Of your standing at water's edge,

Thinking, maybe, *time to go,*
Tall, so tall, in the patient moment.

Blackberry Summer

I love these wild, thorny gifts,
their nuisance ripening
August into something more
than complaints about the heat
and back-to-autumn chores.

I don't mind getting pricked
untangling the dog from low vines
that try to hide their tart secrets.
I'm too selfish to bring a basket
or pail: snatch blackberries singly
and eat them alone, I say.

If I were my mother, I'd make
the house think for two days
about hot water, spilled sugar,
and the art of sealing jars,
before sharing my jelly with the world,

but I've left such charity behind.
Bad luck and bad character taught me
to seize the blackberry: out here,
it's every Tom, squirrel, and sparrow
for himself, baby, and this poem
is close as you'll get to my blackberry luck.

Bowls

Aunt Marian's wooden canoe for biscuit making,
Or the orphan from a wedding pair;

Miss Polly's seasick white one
That shows off fruit salad,

Mama's fifty-cents Baptist special
With veggies painted

In the squares of a blue-sash plaid.
I don't have a life any more equal to these:

Divorce, cats as an occupying force,
The apartment with Seventies lights and carpet.

Who needs these dusty burdens
At sixty and counting?

Life is a matter of letting go
Read the sampler

I gave to the church rummage sale.
My cousin the hoarder would take

The bowls and their stories,
Plus anything else that would occupy

Her need for proof that we were here.
Yet I seem to be just as bad,

A cracked southern queen defeated
By nostalgia for what was and never was.

So I wash my annoying treasures
In Dawn, like babies or oil-slicked birds,

Curator for the dead and my estate sale:
Free irony.

Akron Rain in Late Middle Age

I've got Lena Home on the ancient turntable
Singing *The Man I Love* as if there were only one,

While the poodle refuses to let me stop
Rubbing her belly bigger than our lives.

Neither of us does what's expected anymore,
Especially this afternoon as rain draws

Curtains on what's left of the world.
Nostalgia wants to rise from the carpet,

But I get the bug spray to take care of that.
Let's hear it for losing your resume

And the words *success* and *achievement* forever.
Three boxes of certificates, awards, and diplomas

Sleep in deserved dust as I work this glass of Malbec
Large enough to float my life. Let's toast biweekly trips

To the library and West Point Market for more wine
and cheese: I'm afraid those who want to get ahead, will,

But I can't save them from promotions and praise.
I call now for the time and weather to read

Old letters out loud, to remember Mama saying
Her psychiatrist in Florida told her *your child is good*

For you. I stroll the towpath to visit
Turtles in their rows, beavers on their backs,

And blue herons posing in modernist lines.
These luminous days have no room for iPhones

Or speed reading in airports. I'll sit here,
Beside the pineapple lamp with art books,

Doorstop novels by Henry James.
Daddy told me, *Son, I'm glad*

You can read and figger thangs out, and today
So am I, so am I.

Tibetan Prayer Flags in Holmes County, Ohio

(for Leo)

Wild as summer violets, they hang
like God's laundry between two barns,
slapping the wind in holy union.
They say the Daily Office
and breathe with Mennonites,
find singing lambs for the Lord.
Red and yellow, black and white,
they flirt with geese heading south.

Someone's wandering brother sent them
with God's apology and a prayer wheel
that turns the stream.
Confined to duty, they dance
in Anabaptist dreams,
faith almost in flight.

Notes

Try Me is the title of a ballad recorded by James Brown.

Gospels from the Lower Shelf ends with a line that echoes a song recorded
      by Patsy Cline*: (He Called Me) Baby, Baby All Night Long.*

Many Bright Mansions Above takes its title from an old hymn
      In Bright Mansions Above. When writing the poem, I incorrectly
      remembered the title, then decided I preferred my version.

My Buddy is the title of a popular song; also, the poem ends with a line
      that echoes the title of Leonard Michaels' short story collection
      I Would Have Saved Them If I Could.

Acknowledgments

"Ohio Farm Boy" appeared in *Barn Owl Review*
"Marriage Blanc" appeared in *Rubbertop Review*
"Gospels from the Lower Shelf" appeared in *New Orleans Review*
"I Need from You an Advisement" appeared in *Tar River Poetry*
"Abiding Light," "For the Queens Who Dragged Marlene's Furs Across My Life, and "Mrs. Bendremer" appeared in *The South Carolina Review*
"Knives" appeared in *Plainsongs*
"Etudes for El Paso and Spanish Guitar" appeared in *RHINO*
"October in Richfield, Ohio" appeared in *Penguin Review*
"Odella, at Eighty" appeared in *The Texas Review*
"A Horticulturalist's Guide to Marriage Equality in Ohio" appeared in *The Connecticut Poetry Review* under a slightly different title
"Many Bright Mansions Above" appeared in *Ohio Writer*
"Try Me" and "Coyotes Walk Up Oakdale Street on Christmas Eve" appeared in *Whiskey Island Magazine*
"A Woman Bathes in the Ohio River," "Stealing Lumber on Sunday Afternoon," and "Guys with Their Hands in Their Pockets" appeared in *Muse*
"New Thinking on How to Protect the Heart" and "Hawk in December" appeared in *Jelly Bucket*
"Red Onions" and "Bowls" appeared in *The Comstock Review*
"Before the Rapture Comes" and "Brandywine Falls in June" appeared in *Front Range Review*
"The Sewing Circle and Altar Guild of St. Michael's Episcopal Church" appeared in *Colere*

A seventh-generation southerner, **Thomas Dukes** was born in Gainesville, Florida, near his father's home in Lake Butler, and grew up in Aiken, South Carolina, near his mother's home in White Pond. After a happy boyhood, he survived an often-troubled adolescence, marked in part by serious illness including a blood disease and Type One Diabetes. Since then, he has lived in what Flannery O'Connor called "the land of the sick." A semester working with disabled children saved his soul.

On whim, at age seventeen, Tom went to The University of Texas at El Paso, from which he managed to graduate with a BA and MA in English (Creative Writing) in spite of enjoying enough of the Seventies to taste the times without its destroying his life. In a fit of madness, he then went to Indiana, Purdue University, where he certainly did not belong, and earned a doctorate in English (Modern Literature) in spite of the conservative Eighties and the rather stolid Midwest.

Hired by The University of Akron as an Assistant Professor, both Akron and he began an economic and spiritual recovery. Tom eventually was promoted to Professor and served in a variety of administrative positions, including Associate Provost. His husband and he were joined in civil union in Vermont in 2000 and married in Canada in 2003. They live in a community between Akron and Cleveland and are ruled by their pets.

www.ingramcontent.com/pod-product-compliance
Lightning Source LLC
Chambersburg PA
CBHW020338170426
43200CB00006B/430